A COLORING BOOK FOR THE EXTREME

COLOR-X

EDITION 1

SKATEBOARDING

COLOR-X

ISBN: 978-0-692-82082-7

For information regarding special sales, giveaways, and bulk purchasing, please contact colorxbooks@gmail.com

Visit us at colorxbooks.com

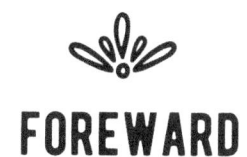

FOREWARD

WELCOME TO COLOR X, THE WORLD'S FIRST ACTION SPORTS COLORING BOOK. A FEW THINGS TO EASE YOU INTO THE IMPENDING EXTREME PAGES: COLOR X IS CURATED, DESIGNED, AND ILLUSTRATED BY THE SKATE INDUSTRY'S TOP PROFESSIONALS... SO DON'T TRY THIS AT HOME. THE IMAGES IN THIS BOOK PORTRAY LEGENDARY MOMENTS: REAL PROS, DOING REAL SKATE TRICKS AS CAPTURED BY WORLD RENOWNED PHOTOGRAPHERS. THE ARTISTS AND ALL INVOLVED ARE VERY PROUD OF THEIR WORK. THEY RISKED THEIR LIVES SO YOU COULD COLOR.

THERAPISTS, TEACHERS, AND MEDICAL PROFESSIONALS TOTALLY ENDORSE THE BOOK, TOO. THEY'VE DEEMED IT BOTH THERAPEUTIC AND COGNITIVELY STIMULATING. SO CHILL OUT, EVEN MOMS BACK COLOR X 'CAUSE IT DOESN'T REQUIRE A HELMET.

COLOR X IS PARTNERED WITH TRANSWORLD MAGAZINE AND OTHER LEADING BRANDS TO BRING YOU A FUN, EXCITING, AND TRULY UNIQUE COLORING EXPERIENCE.

THERE ARE NO RULES OR LIABILITY WAIVERS HERE. SO ENJOY AND COLOR AT YOUR OWN RISK.

GANTRY & GARRETT HILL
LOS ANGELES, CA

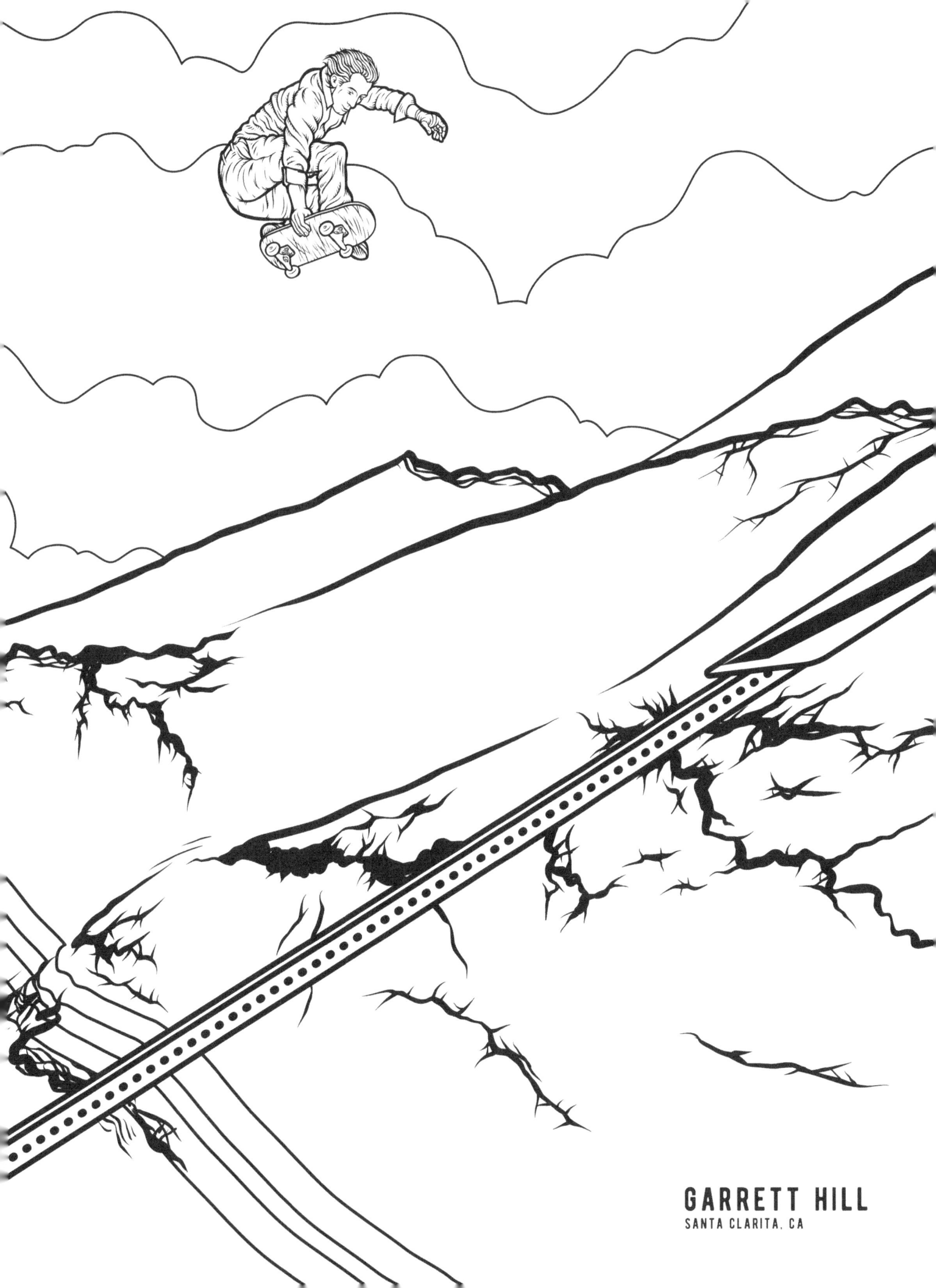

GARRETT HILL
SANTA CLARITA, CA

WORD NERD!

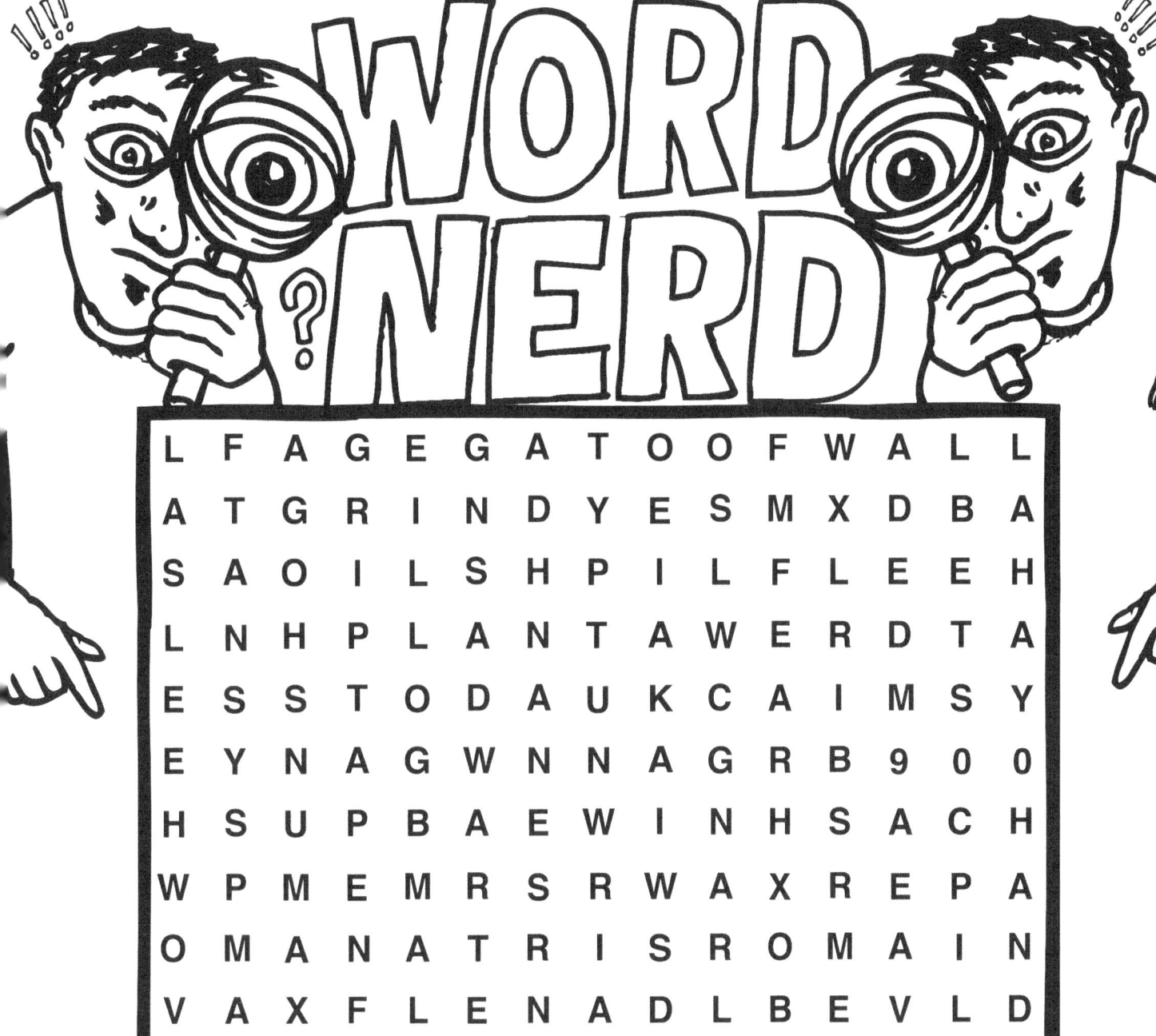

L	F	A	G	E	G	A	T	O	O	F	W	A	L	L
A	T	G	R	I	N	D	Y	E	S	M	X	D	B	A
S	A	O	I	L	S	H	P	I	L	F	L	E	E	H
L	N	H	P	L	A	N	T	A	W	E	R	D	T	A
E	S	S	T	O	D	A	U	K	C	A	I	M	S	Y
E	Y	N	A	G	W	N	N	A	G	R	B	9	0	0
H	S	U	P	B	A	E	W	I	N	H	S	A	C	H
W	P	M	E	M	R	S	R	W	A	X	R	E	P	A
O	M	A	N	A	T	R	I	S	R	O	M	A	I	N
V	A	X	F	L	E	N	A	D	L	B	E	V	L	D
S	R	I	O	S	I	N	G	G	Y	I	E	O	F	R
L	T	B	E	L	A	Y	I	A	Q	Y	D	L	K	A
L	R	E	D	C	U	R	B	N	O	O	W	E	C	I
A	E	S	K	C	G	R	I	Z	Z	L	Y	A	I	L
O	V	T	T	S	E	T	N	O	C	E	R	D	K	O

OLLIE   BOLTS   MANUAL

OLLIE   BOLTS   MANUAL
KICKFLIP   VERT RAMP   RED CURB
PUSH   GNARLY   HEELFLIP
900   GRIPTAPE   GRIND
POWERSLIDE   WAX   CONTEST
BIG AIR   RIDE   FOOTAGE
WHEELS   GRIZZLY   HANDRAIL

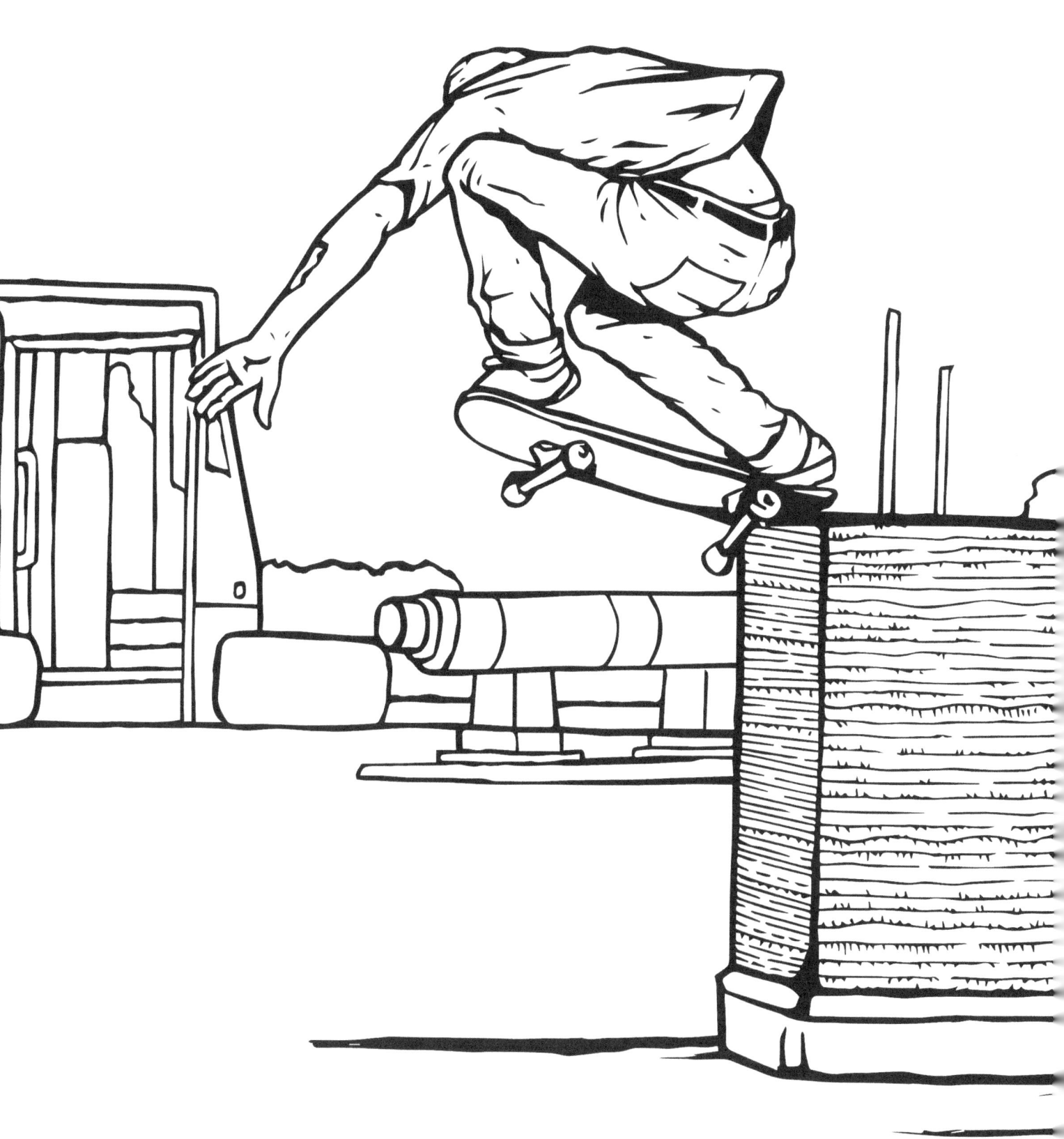

JON DICKSON
ISTANBUL, TURKEY

@metroskateboarding tagged you in a photo.

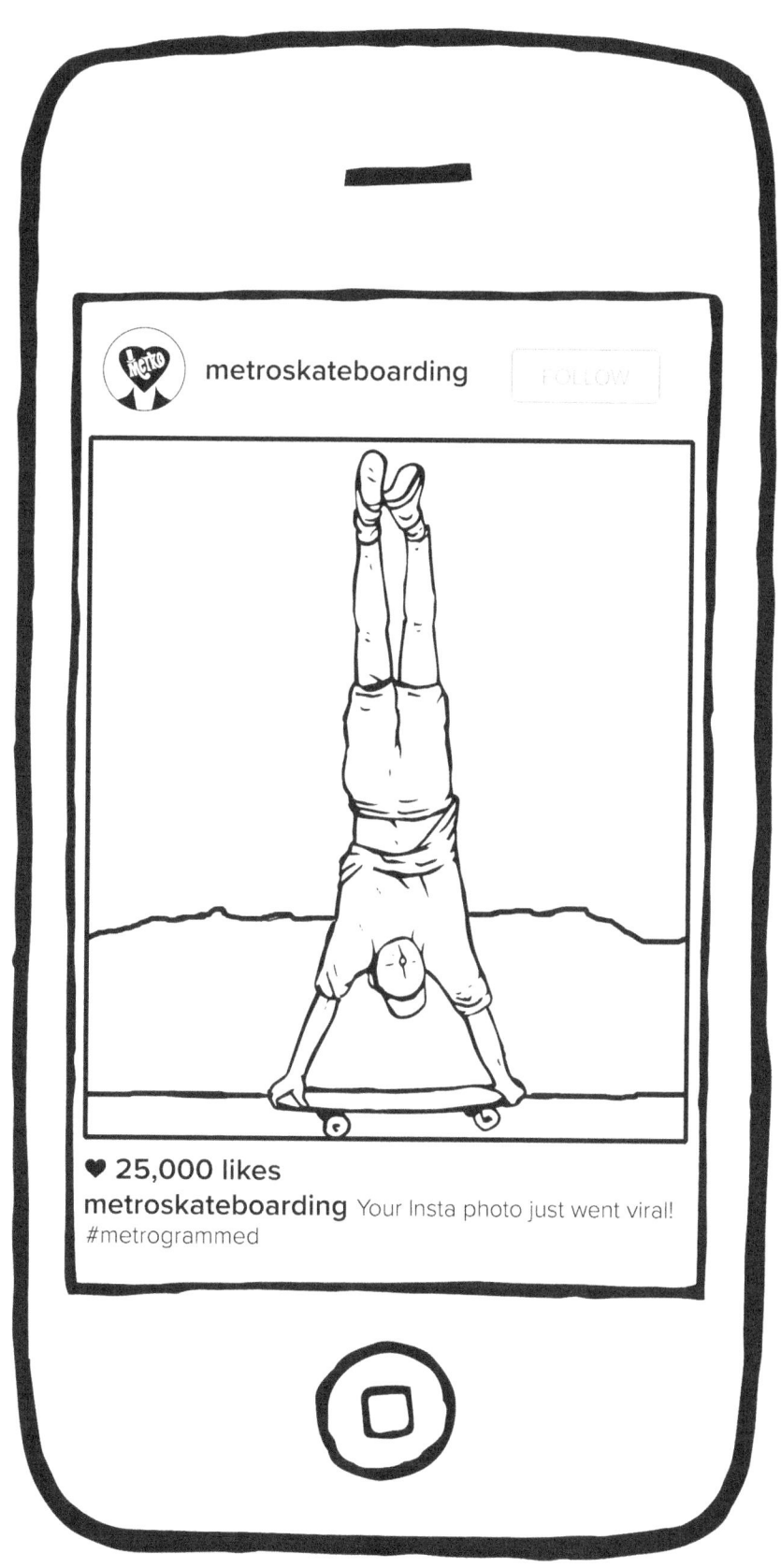

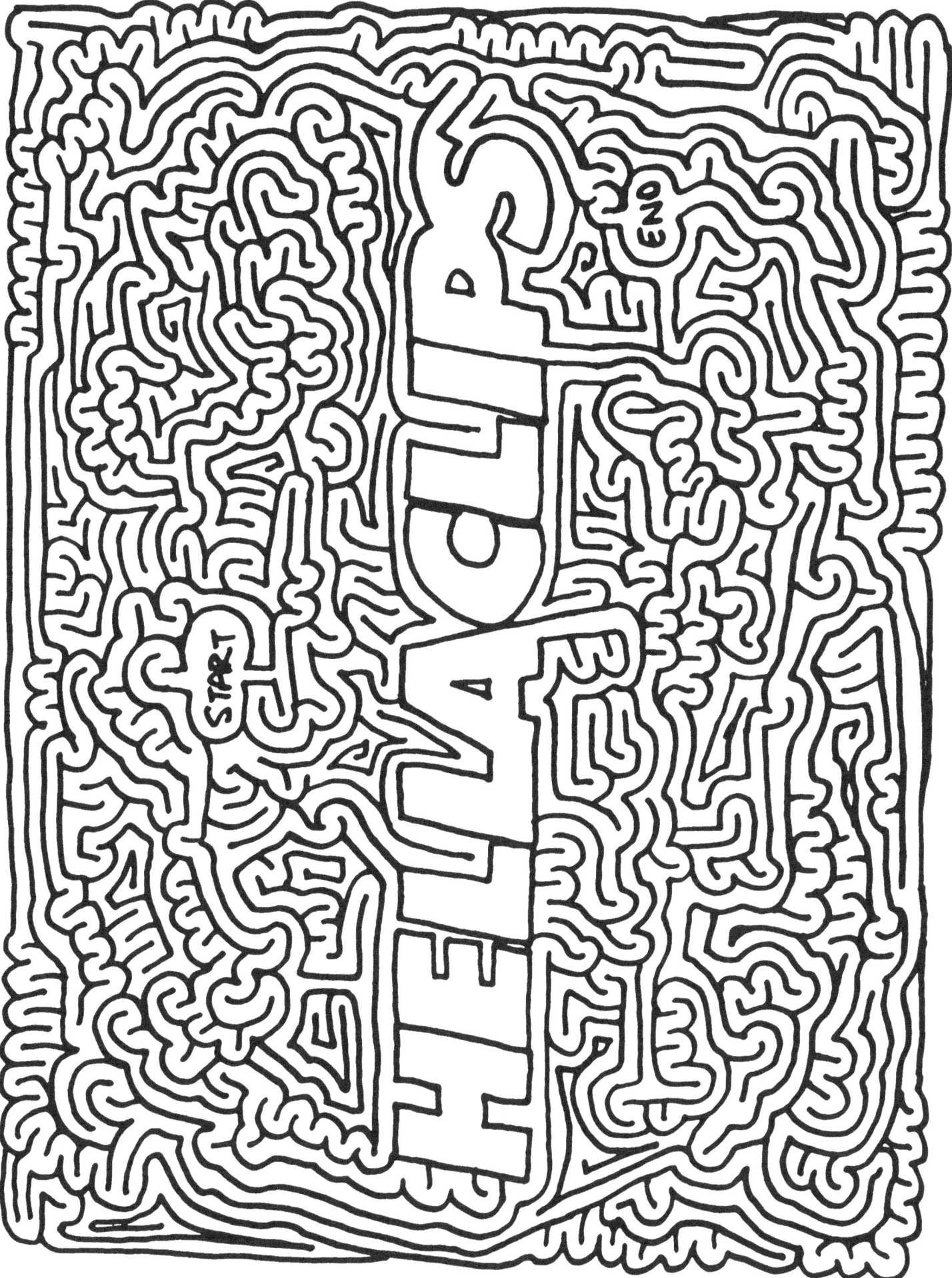

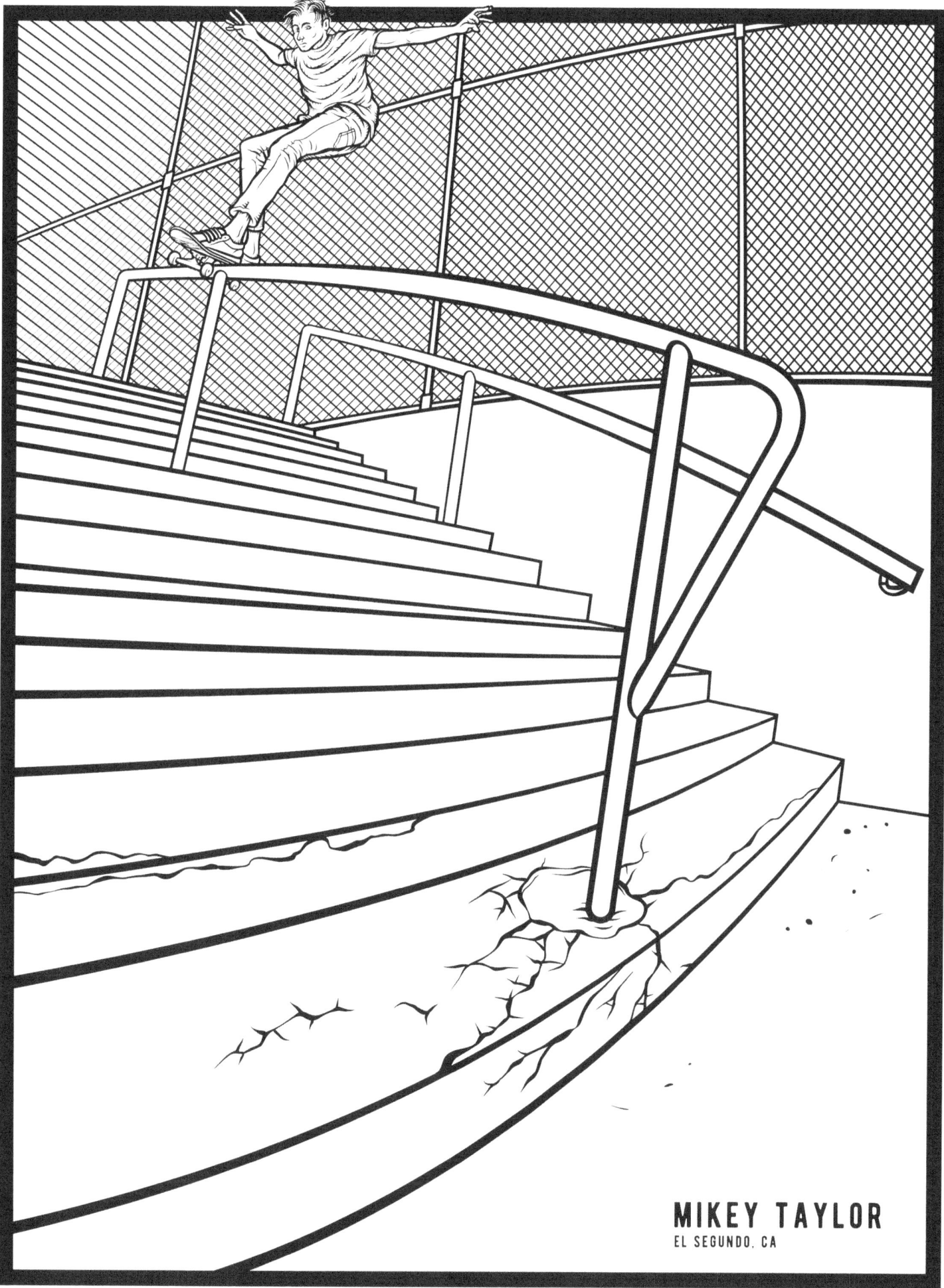

MIKEY TAYLOR
EL SEGUNDO, CA

Connect the dots to complete Slash's beard

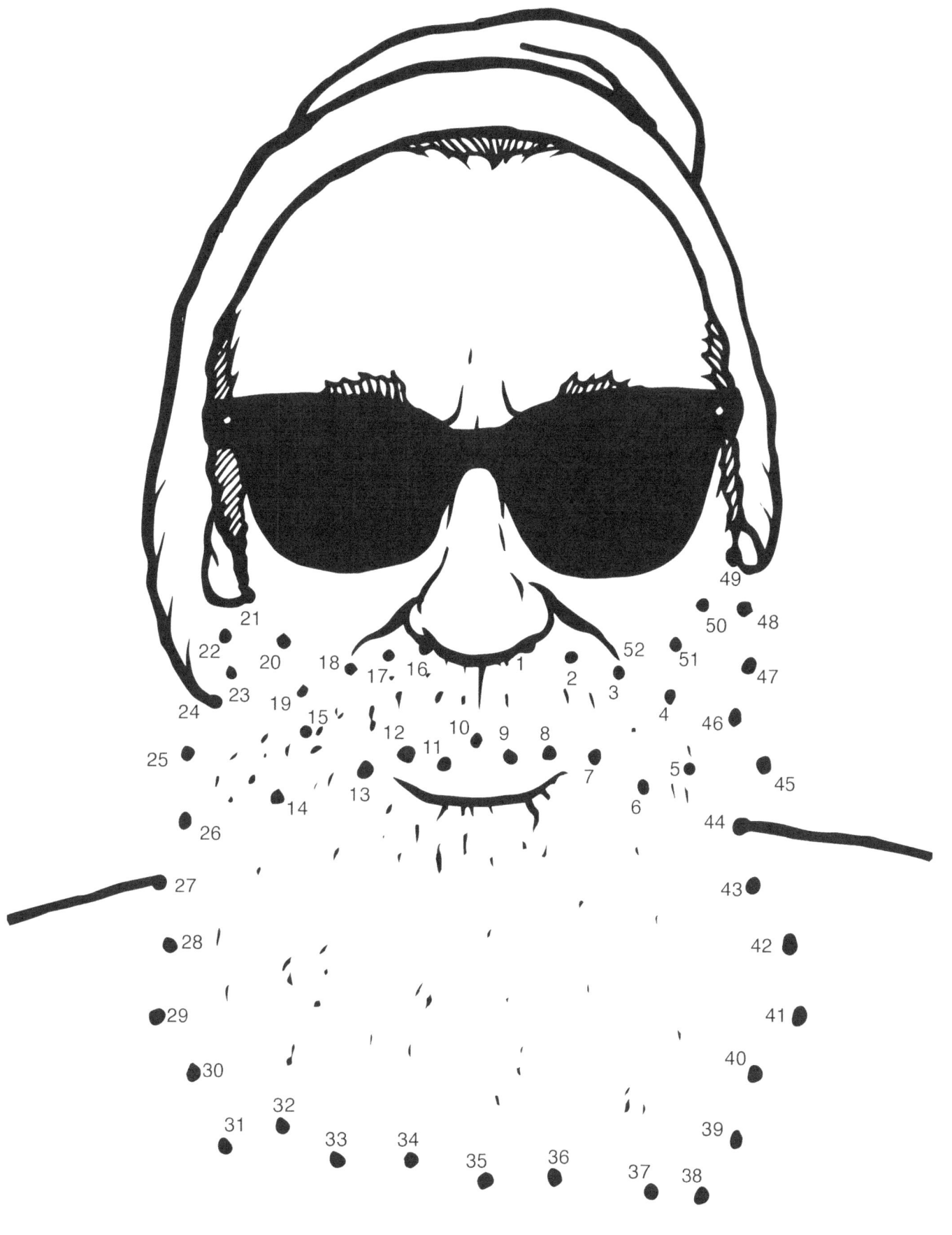

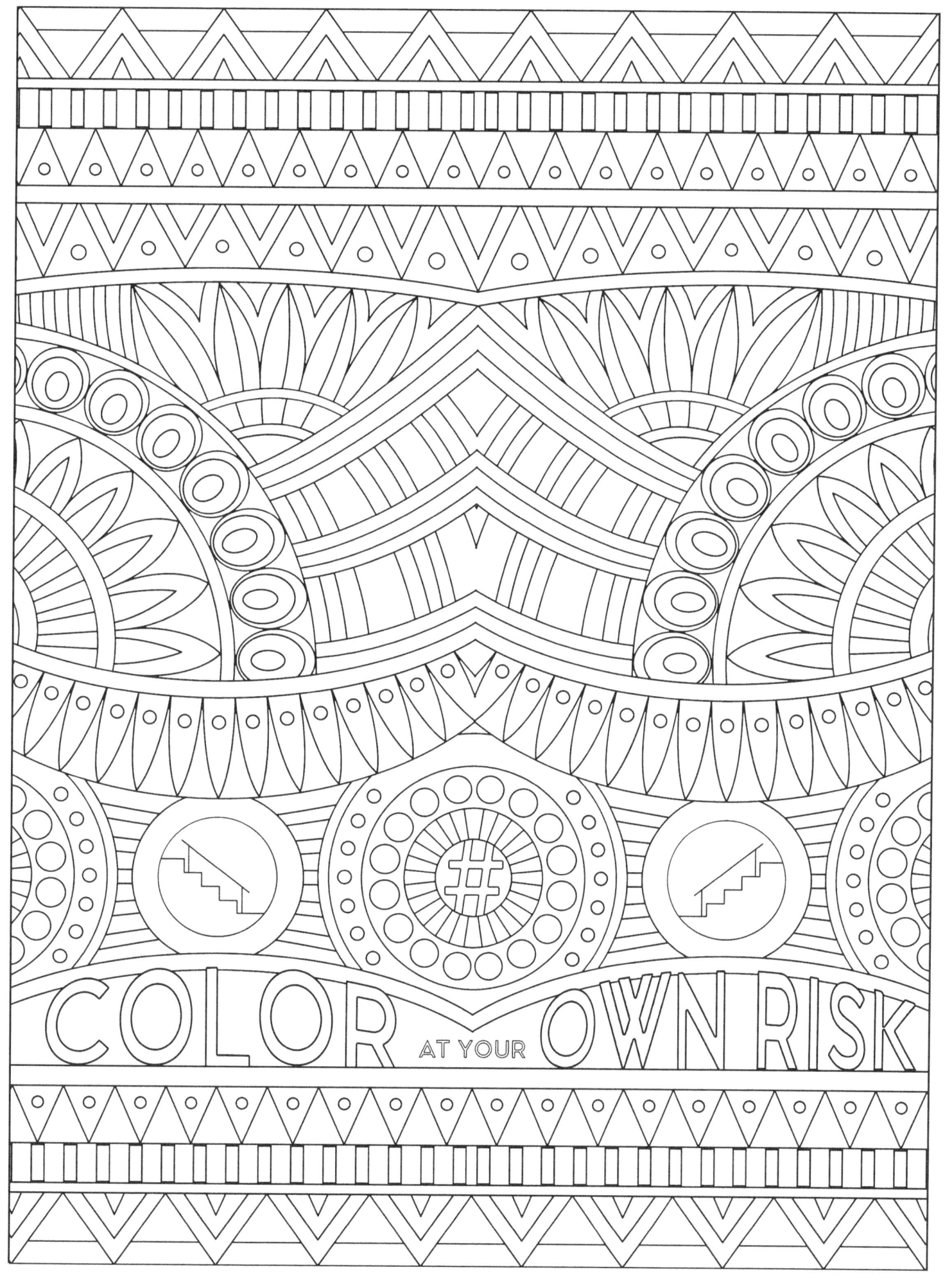

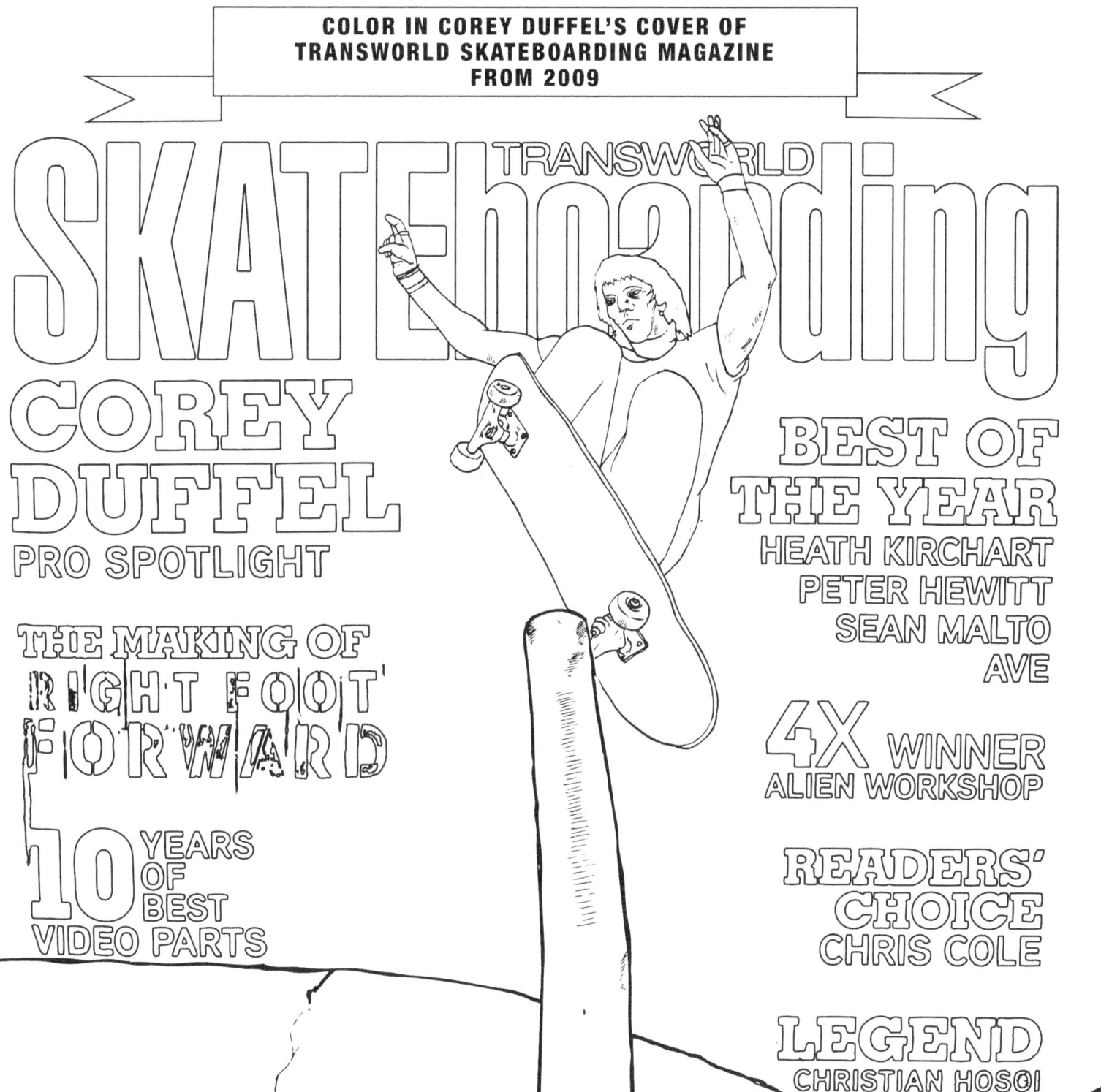

TRANSWORLD
SKATEboarding

COREY
DUFFEL
PRO SPOTLIGHT

THE MAKING OF
RIGHT FOOT
FORWARD

10 YEARS
OF
BEST
VIDEO PARTS

BEST OF
THE YEAR
HEATH KIRCHART
PETER HEWITT
SEAN MALTO
AVE

4X WINNER
ALIEN WORKSHOP

READERS'
CHOICE
CHRIS COLE

LEGEND
CHRISTIAN HOSOI

THE GreatSkate CROSSWORD PUZZLE

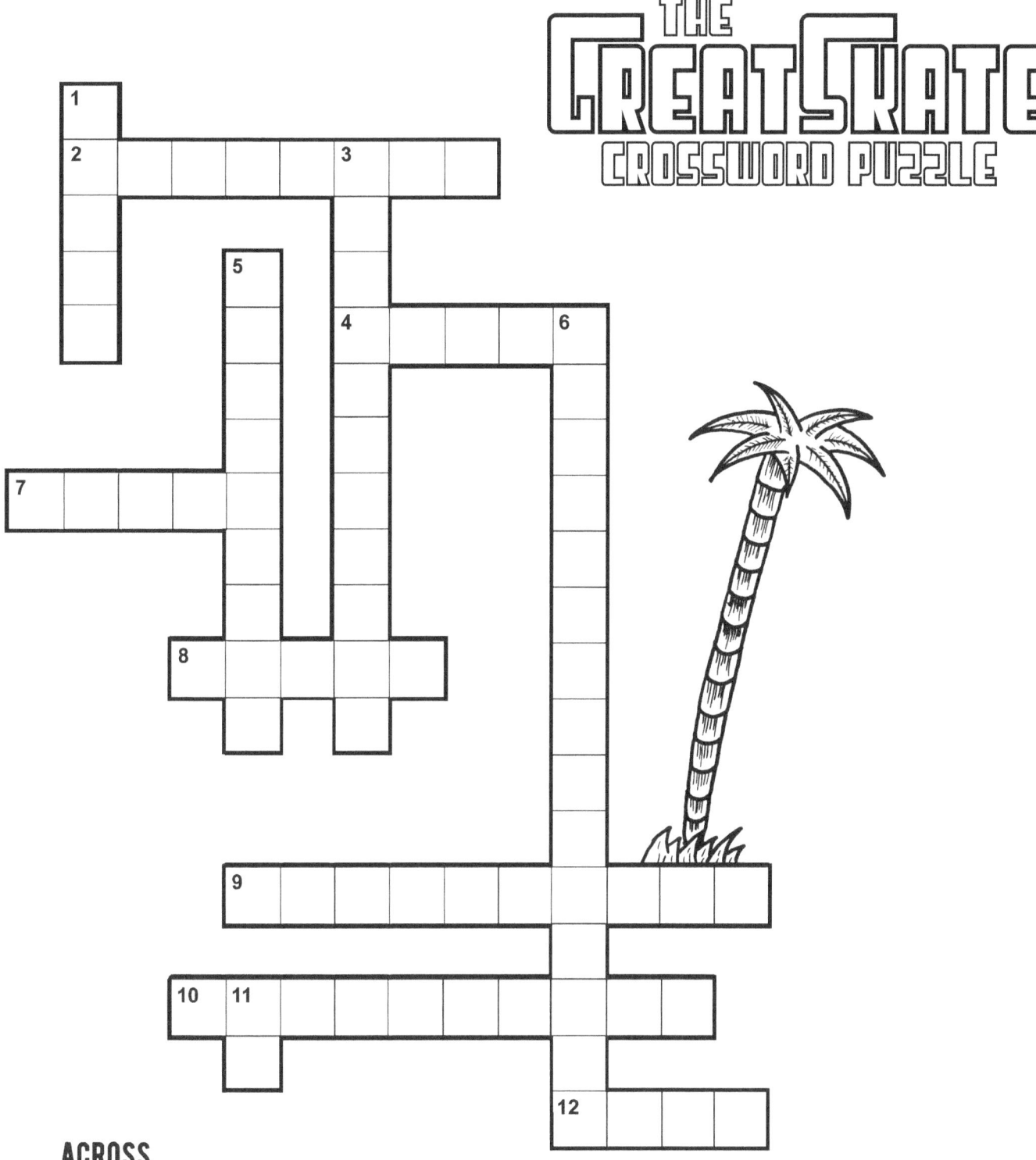

ACROSS

2. FIRST SKATER TO LAND THE 900
4. POPULARIZED THE FAMOUS FIRE HYDRANT SPIN (FIRST NAME)
7. STEEP TERRAIN IN SAN FRANCISCO
8. COMPANY WHO RELEASED THE VIDEO 'QUESTIONABLE'
9. BIRTHPLACE OF SKATEBOARDING (STATE)
10. COMPANY WHO RELEASED THE VIDEO 'GOOD & EVIL'
12. PIONEER/ARTIST WHO HAD A PART IN VIDEO DAYS AND SKATED THE ALCATRAZ PRISON YARD

DOWN

1. PERALTA, OF POWELL-PERALTA
3. INVENTOR OF THE OLLIE
5. SKATER WHO 360 FLIPPED WALLENBERG
6. ORIGINAL NICKNAME FOR SKATEBOARDING
11. "SKATE ___ DIE"

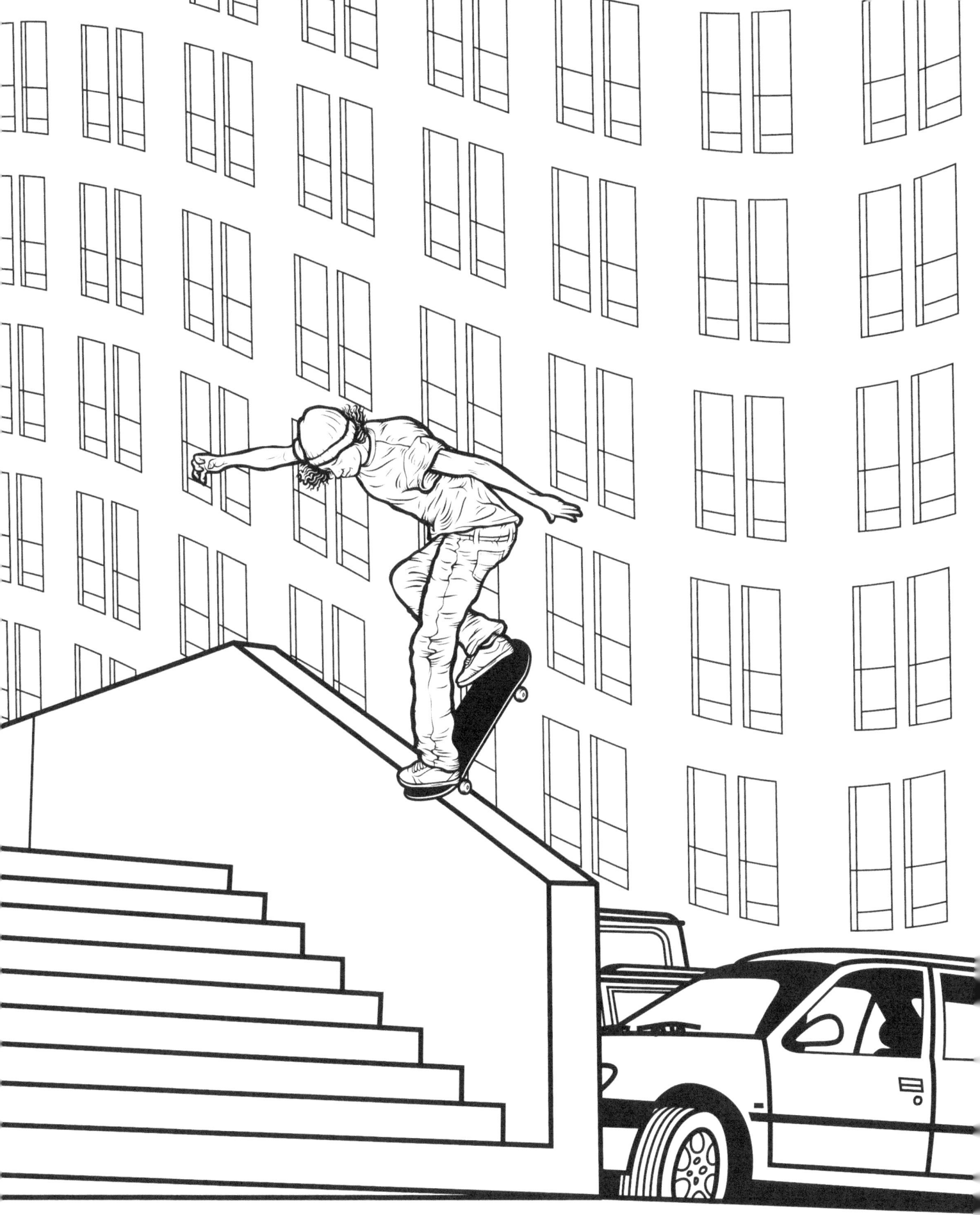

TOM ASTA
LISBON, PORTUGAL

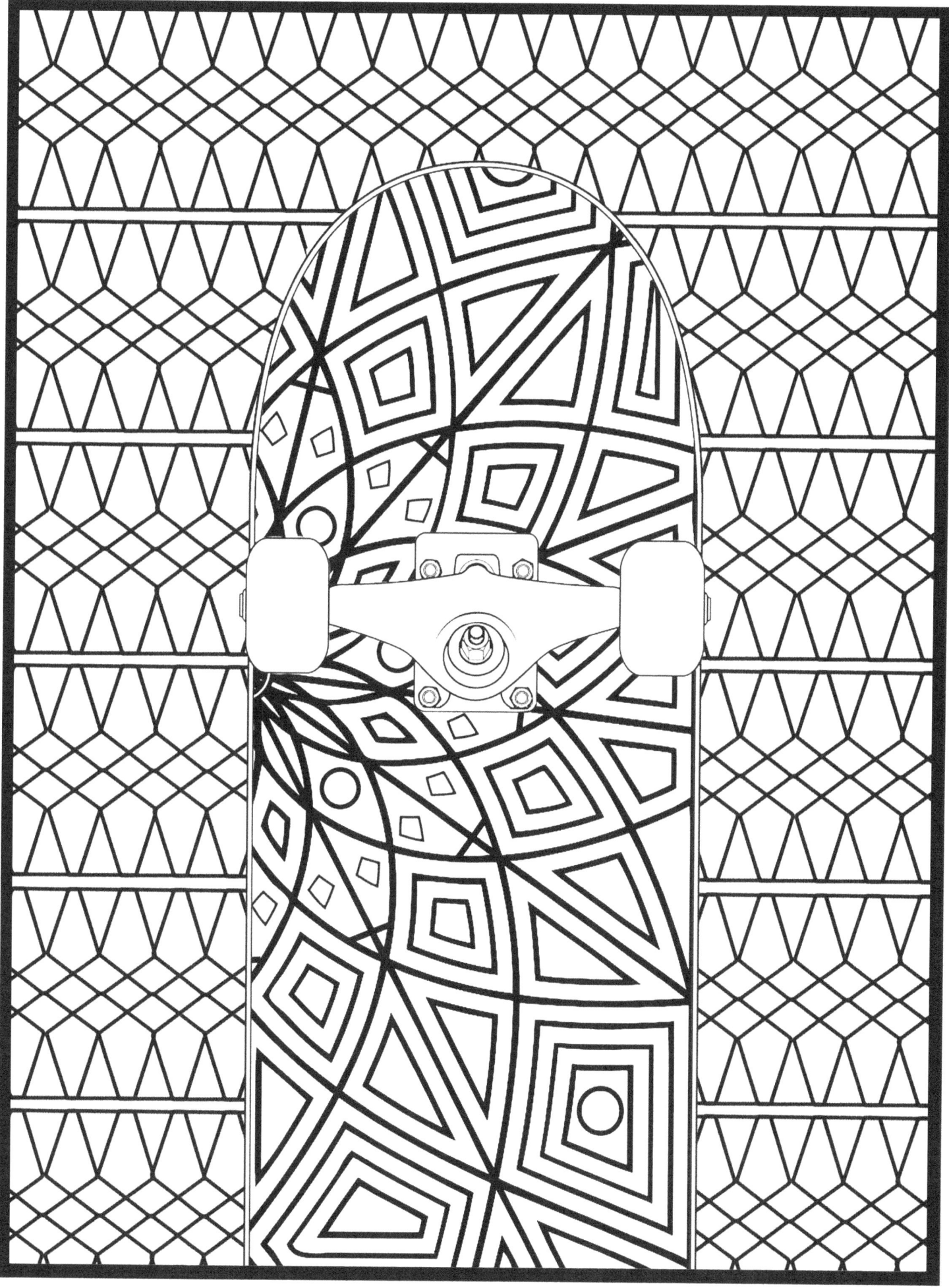

YOU JUST TURNED PRO!!!#:

DESIGN YOUR PRO MODEL BOARD

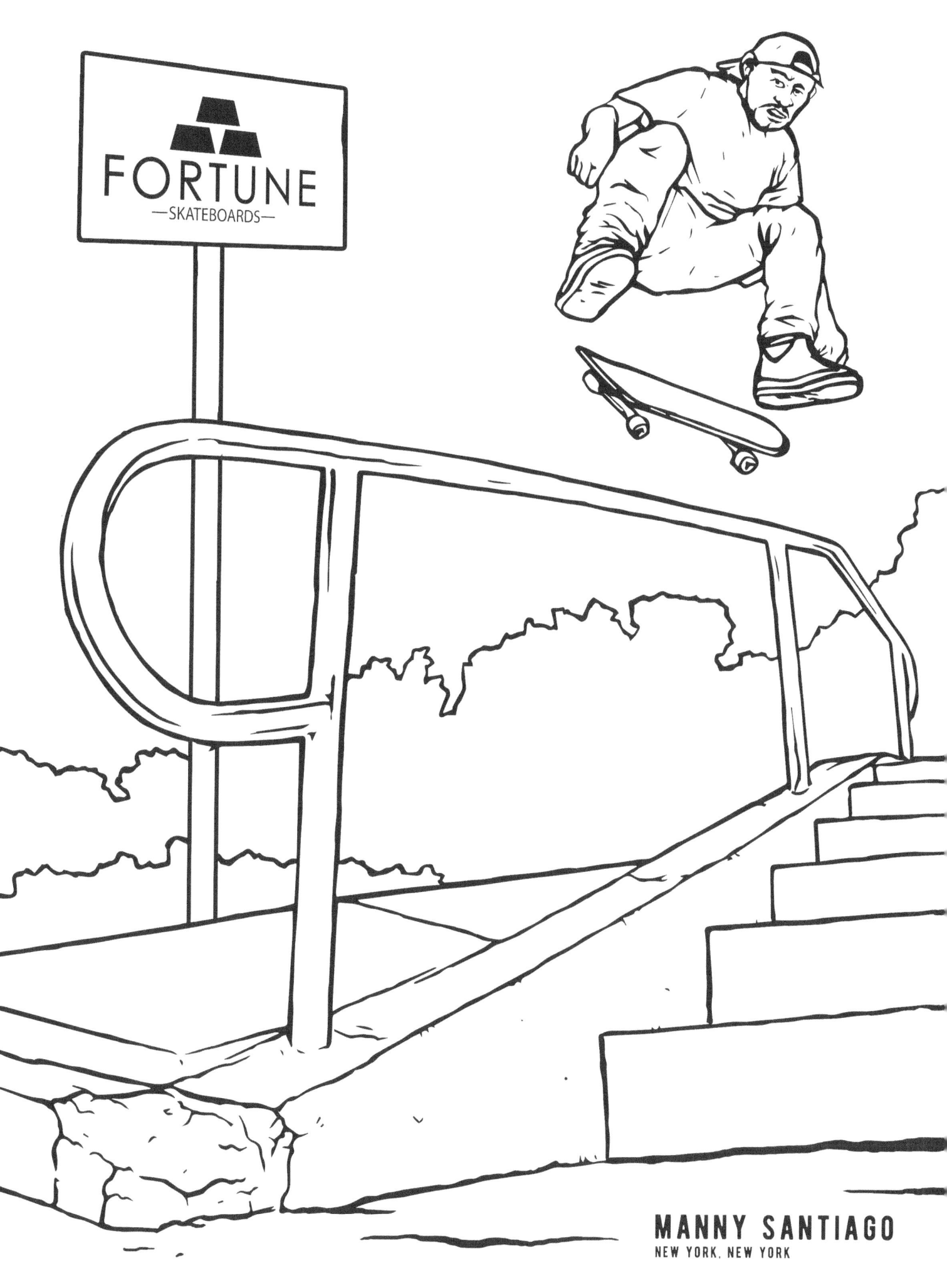

MANNY SANTIAGO
NEW YORK, NEW YORK

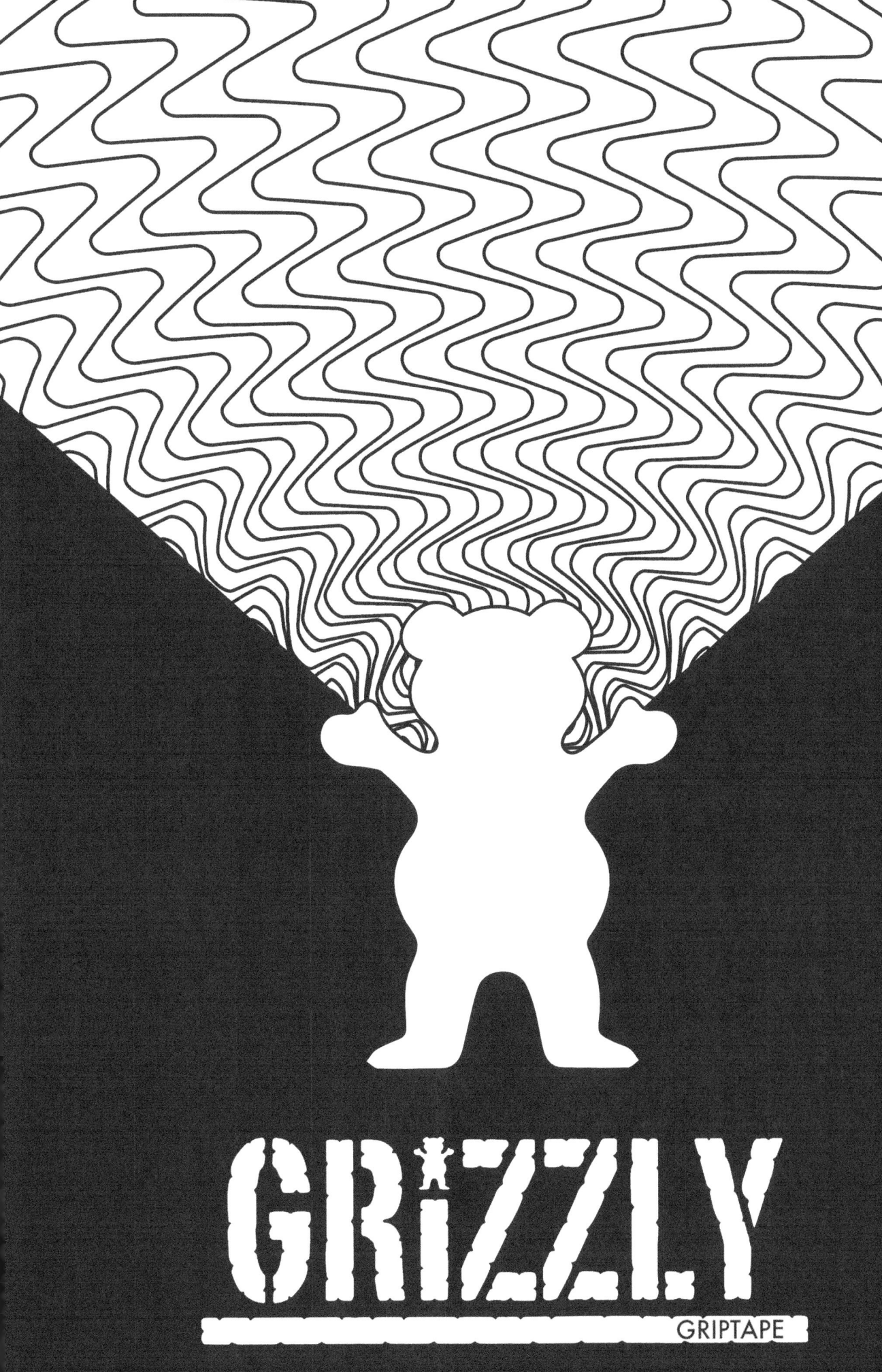

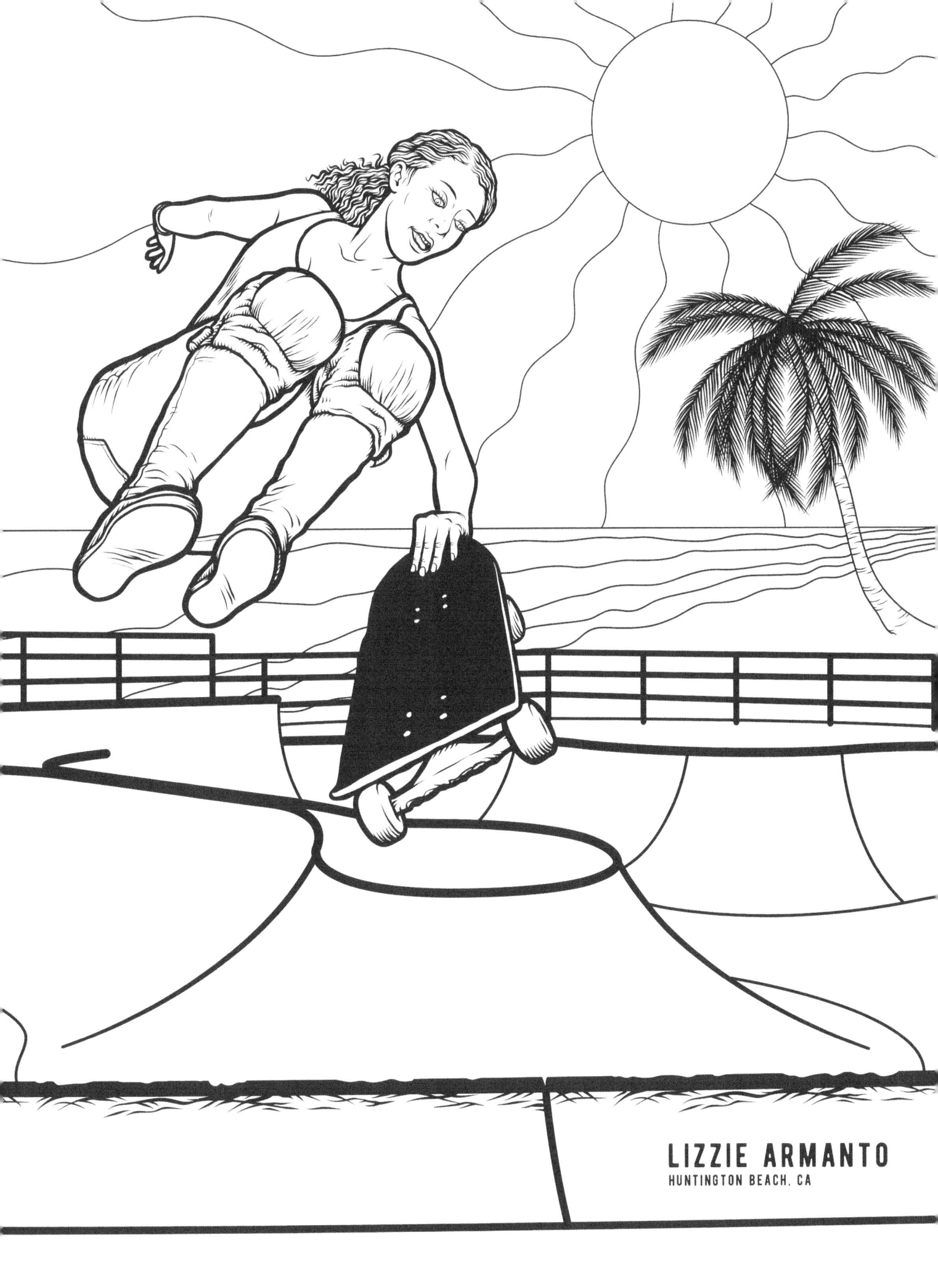

LIZZIE ARMANTO
HUNTINGTON BEACH, CA

ROLL CALL

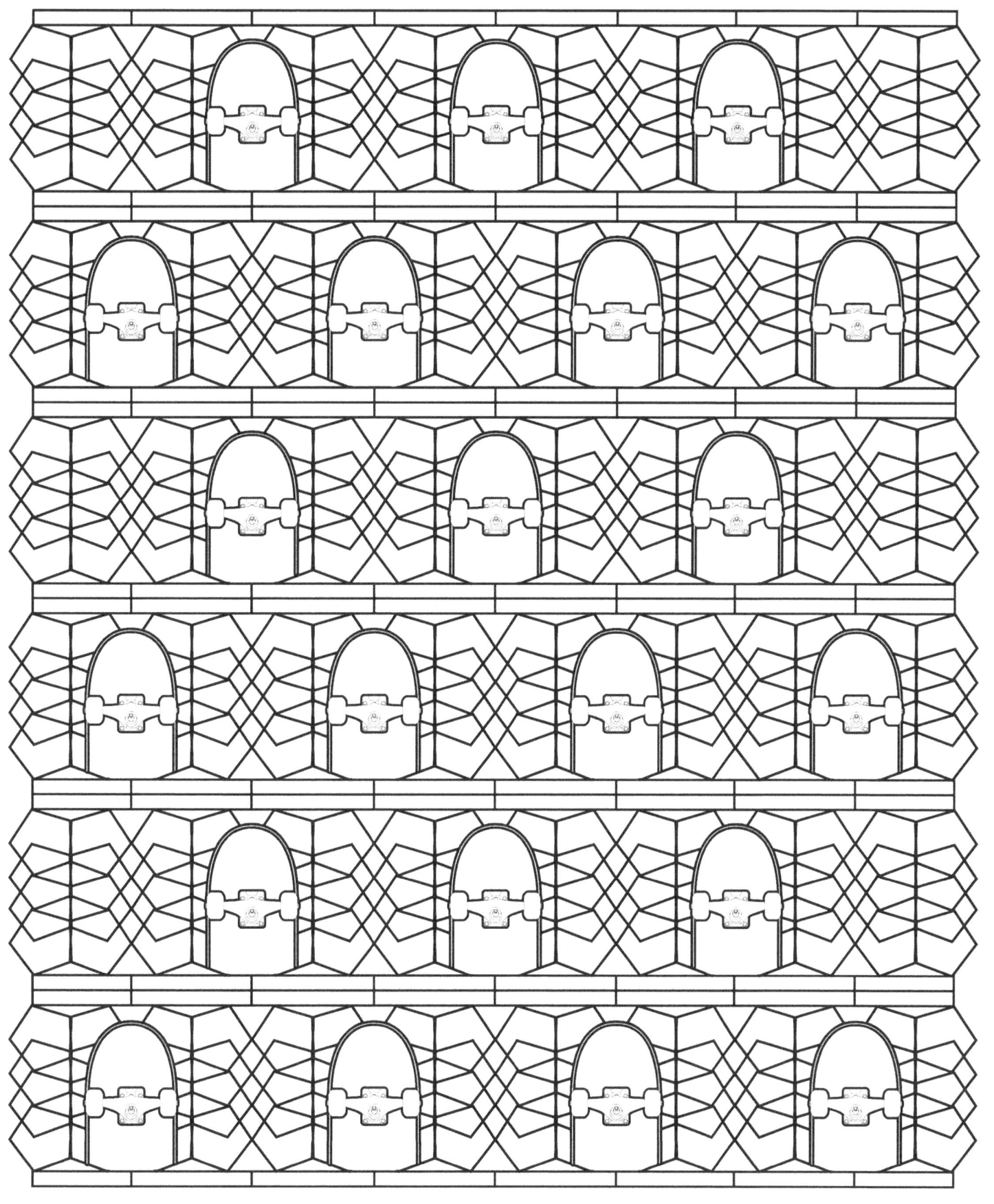

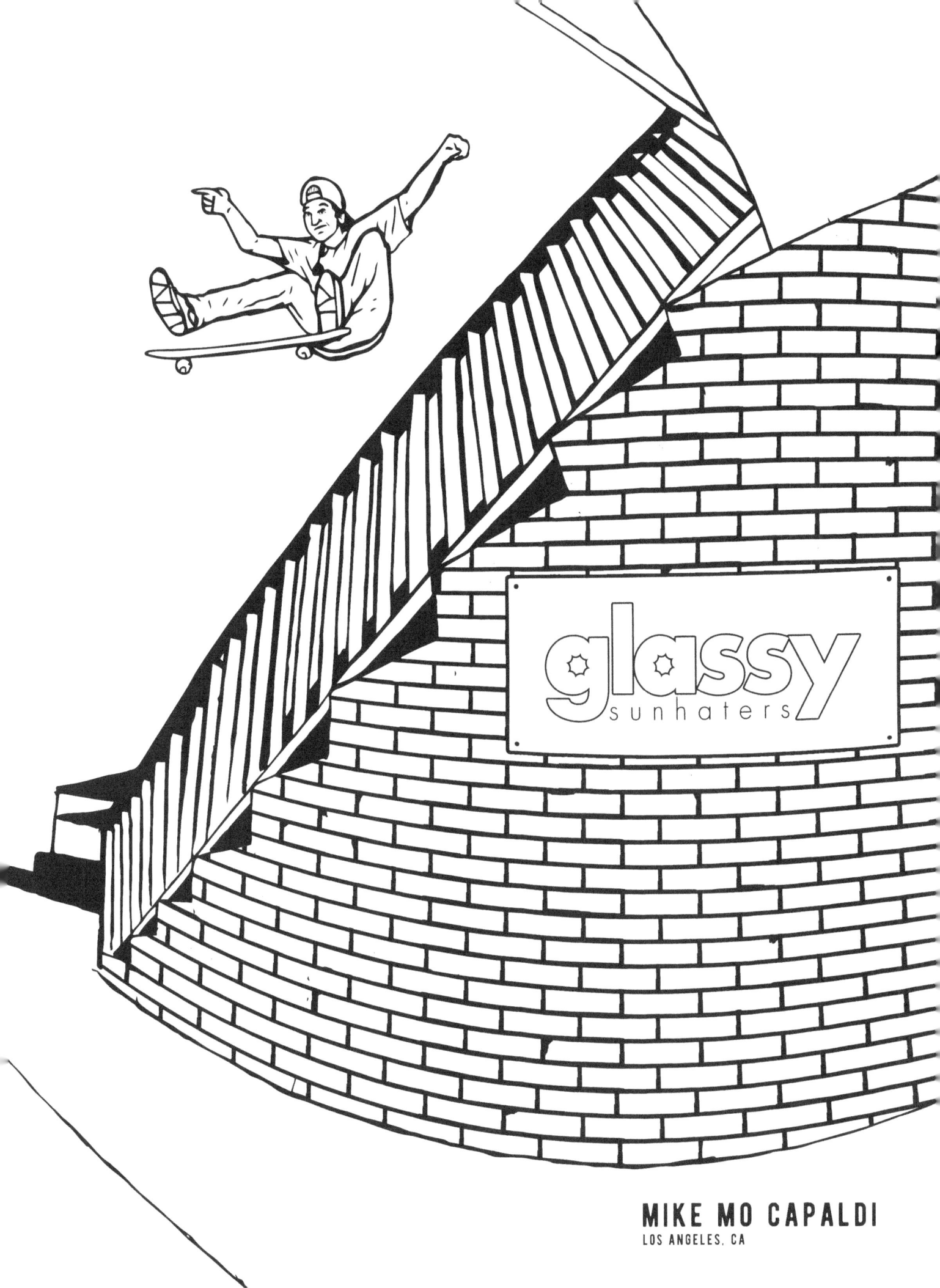

MIKE MO CAPALDI
LOS ANGELES, CA

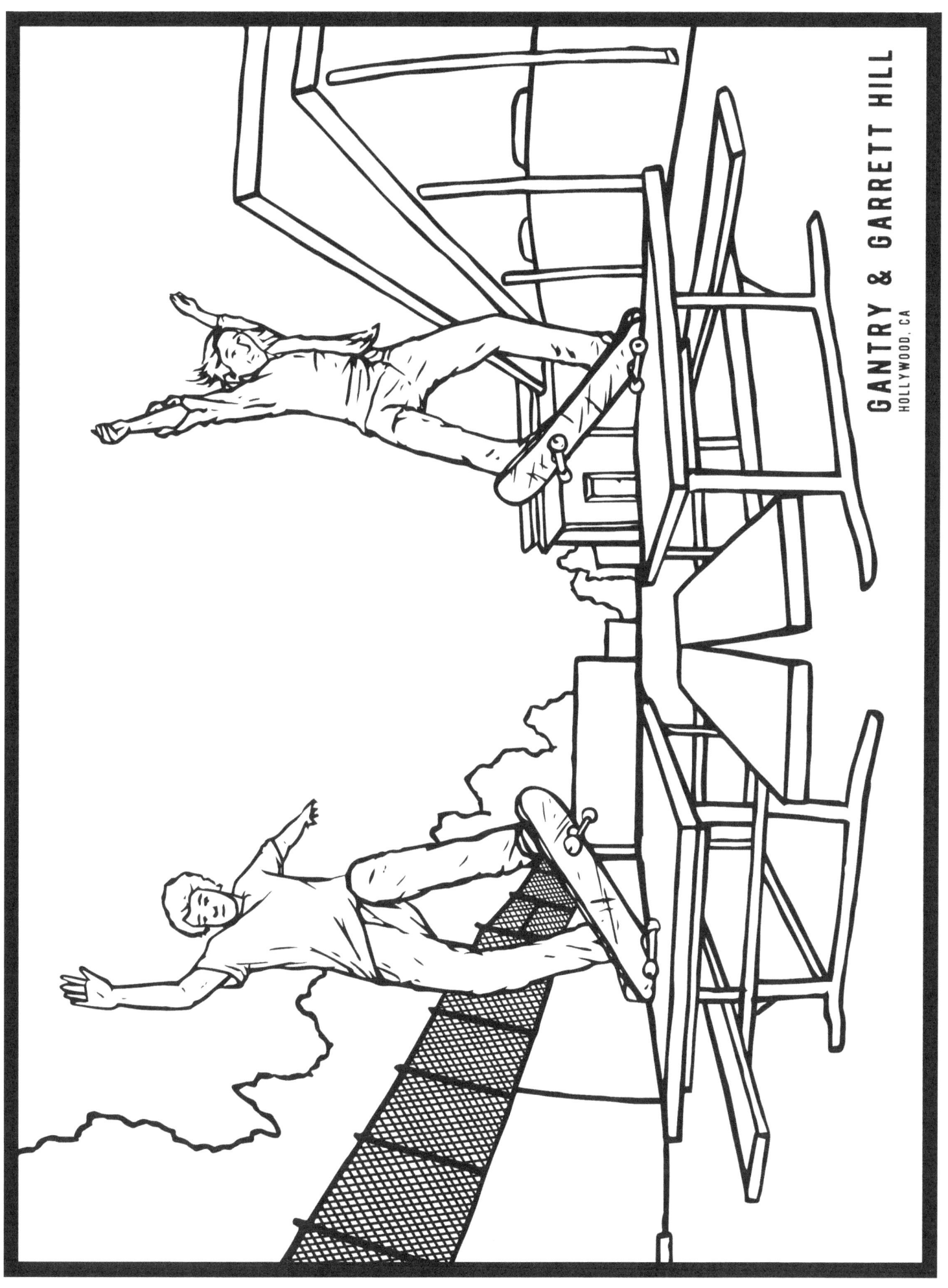

GANTRY & GARRETT HILL

HOLLYWOOD, CA

THE SKATE SCRAMBLE

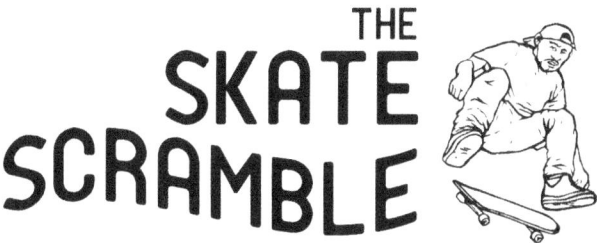

UNSCRAMBLE THE SKATEPARK OBSTACLES

RAFBALT   _____

MPIYDAR   _____

MAIRNPMI   _____

DEEGL   _____

OBX   _____

NLIARADH   _____

IRSTSA   _____

PHI   _____

BUABH   _____

WOBL   _____

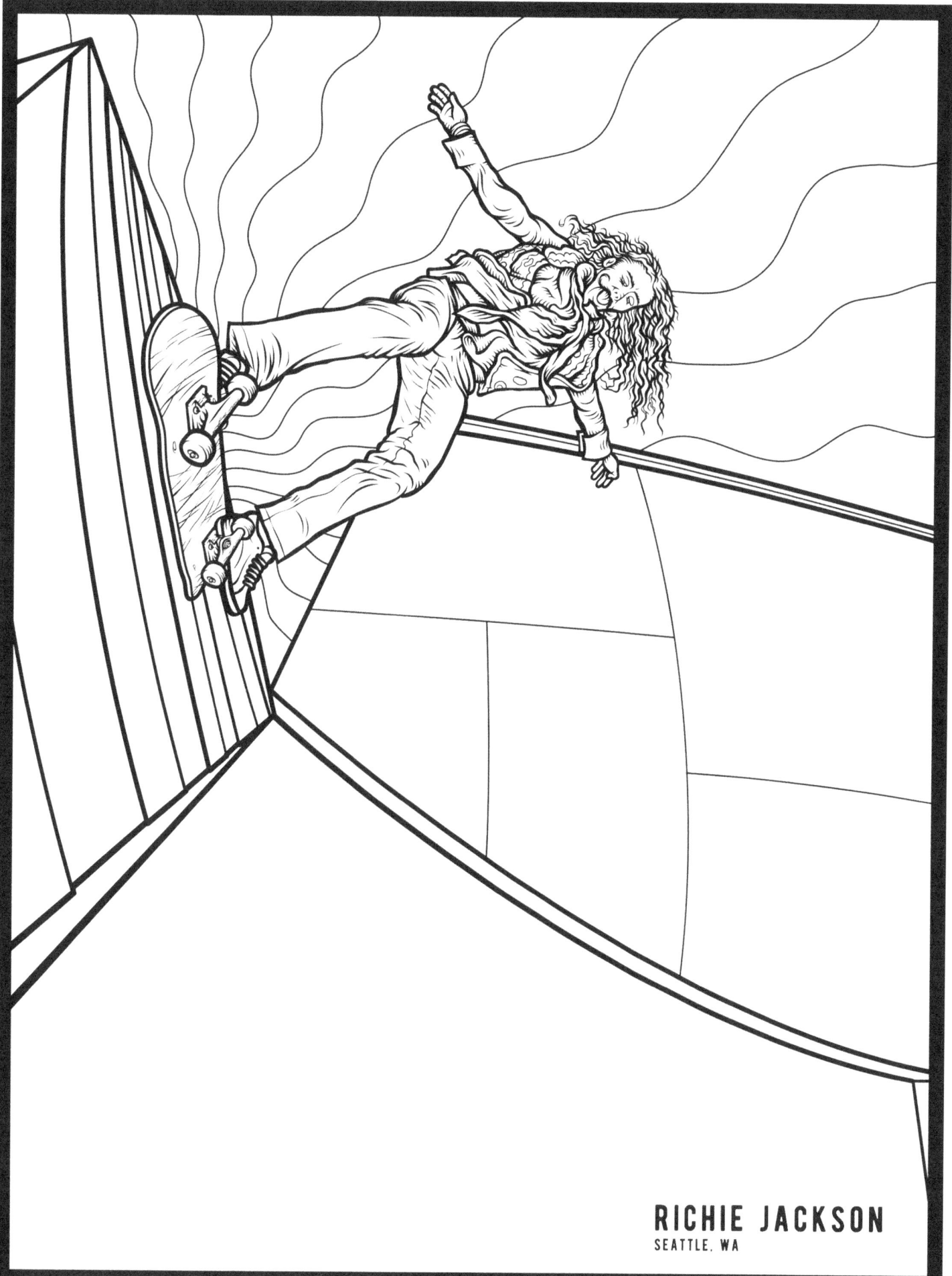

RICHIE JACKSON
SEATTLE, WA

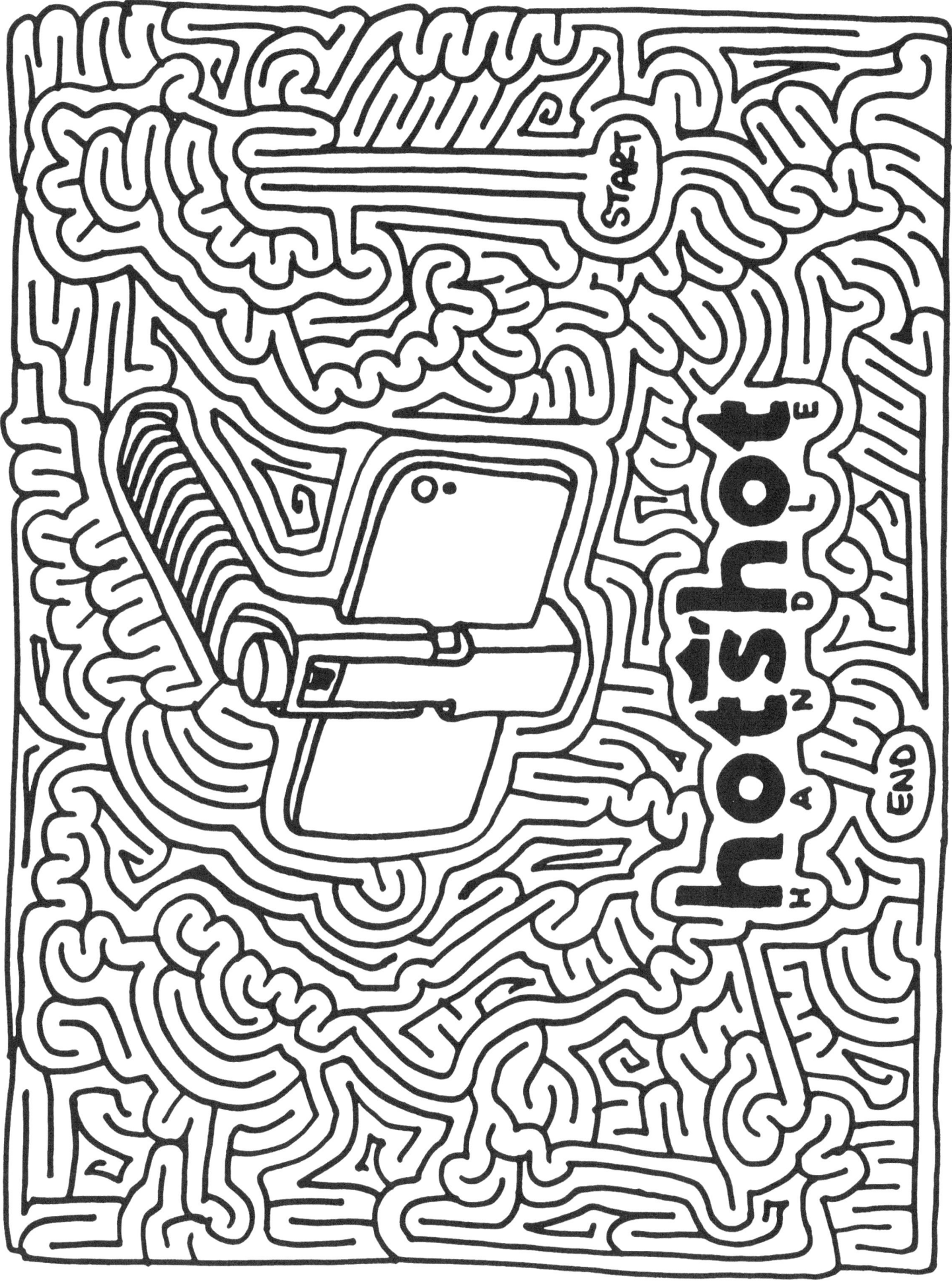

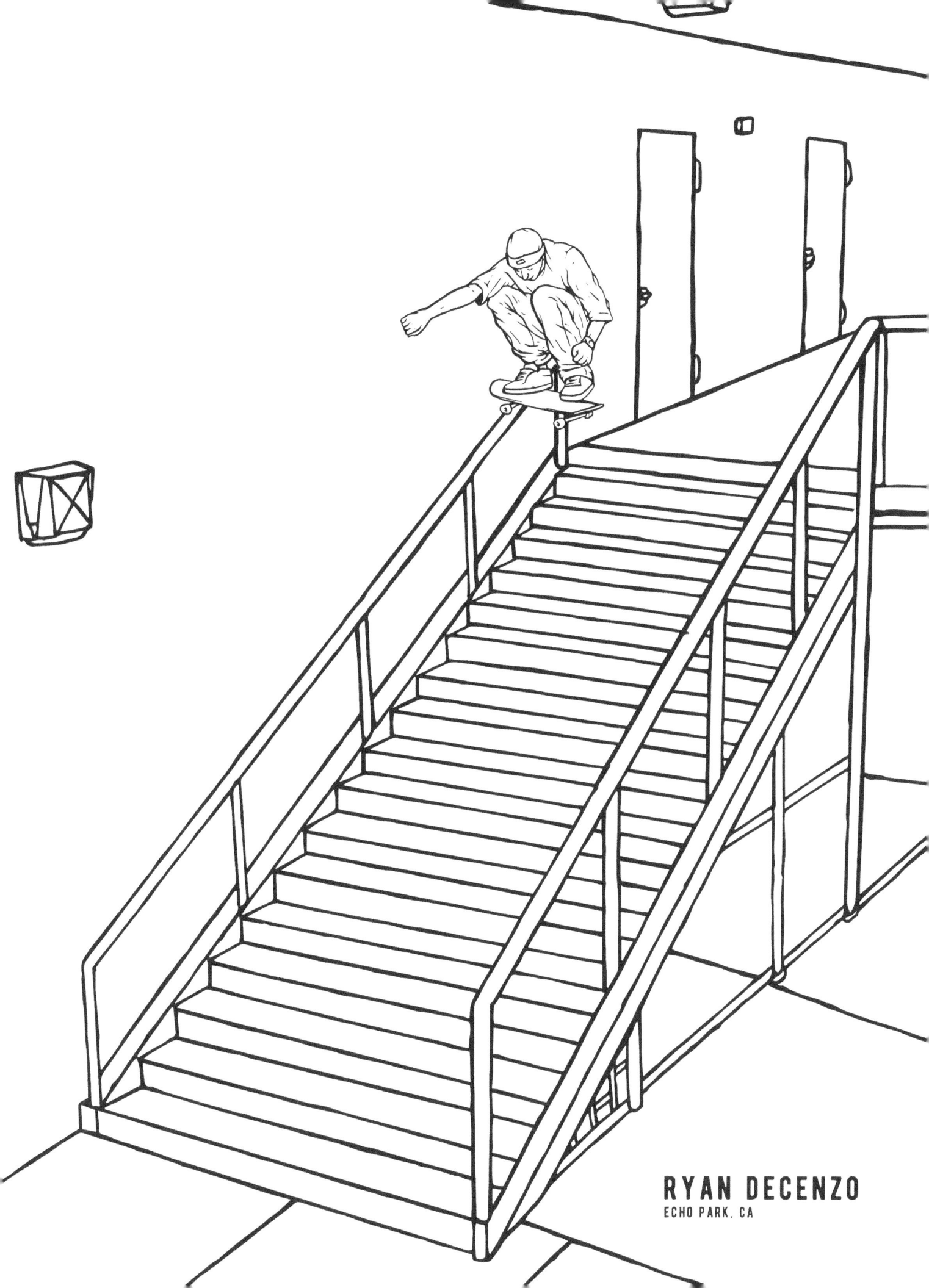

RYAN DECENZO
ECHO PARK, CA

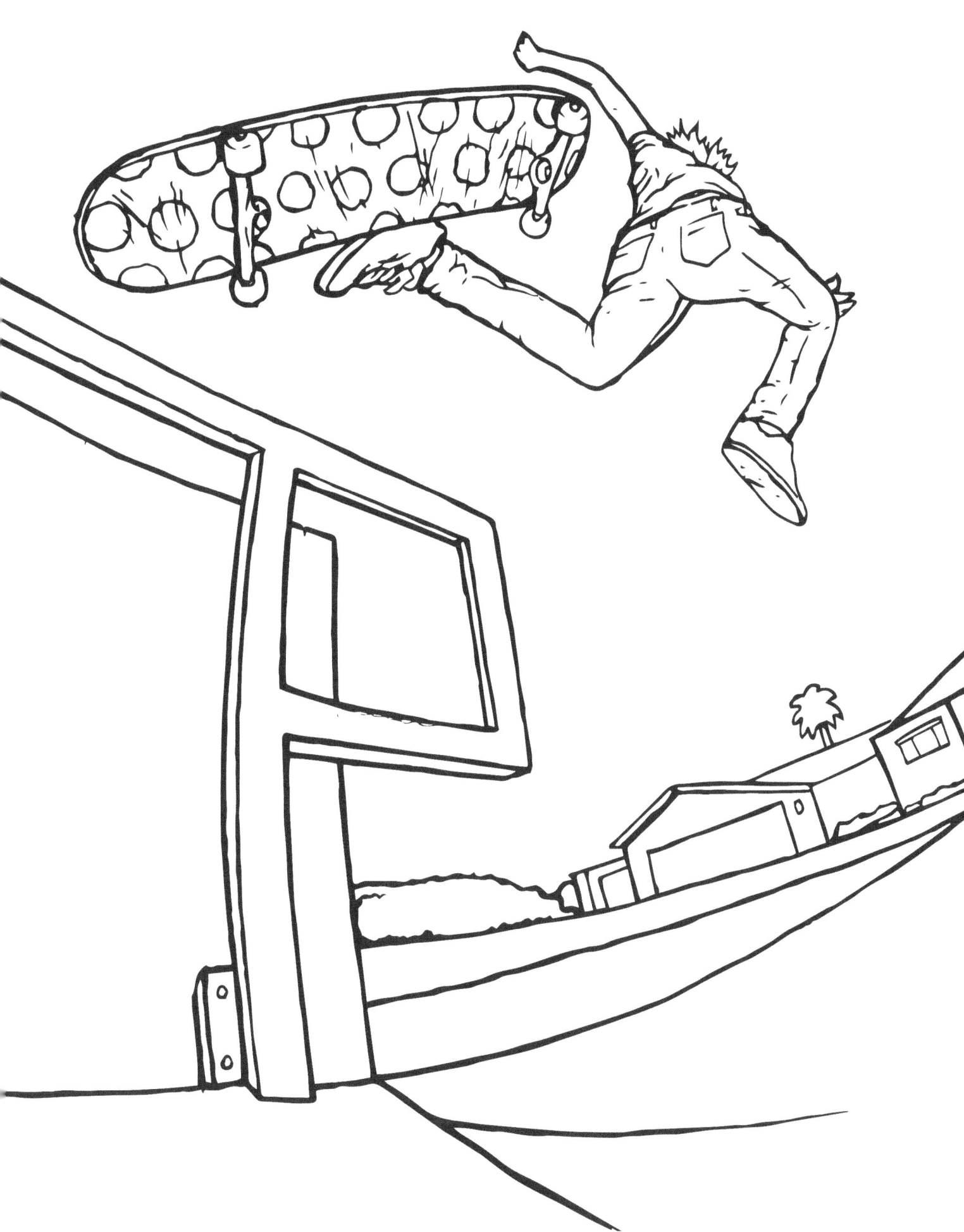

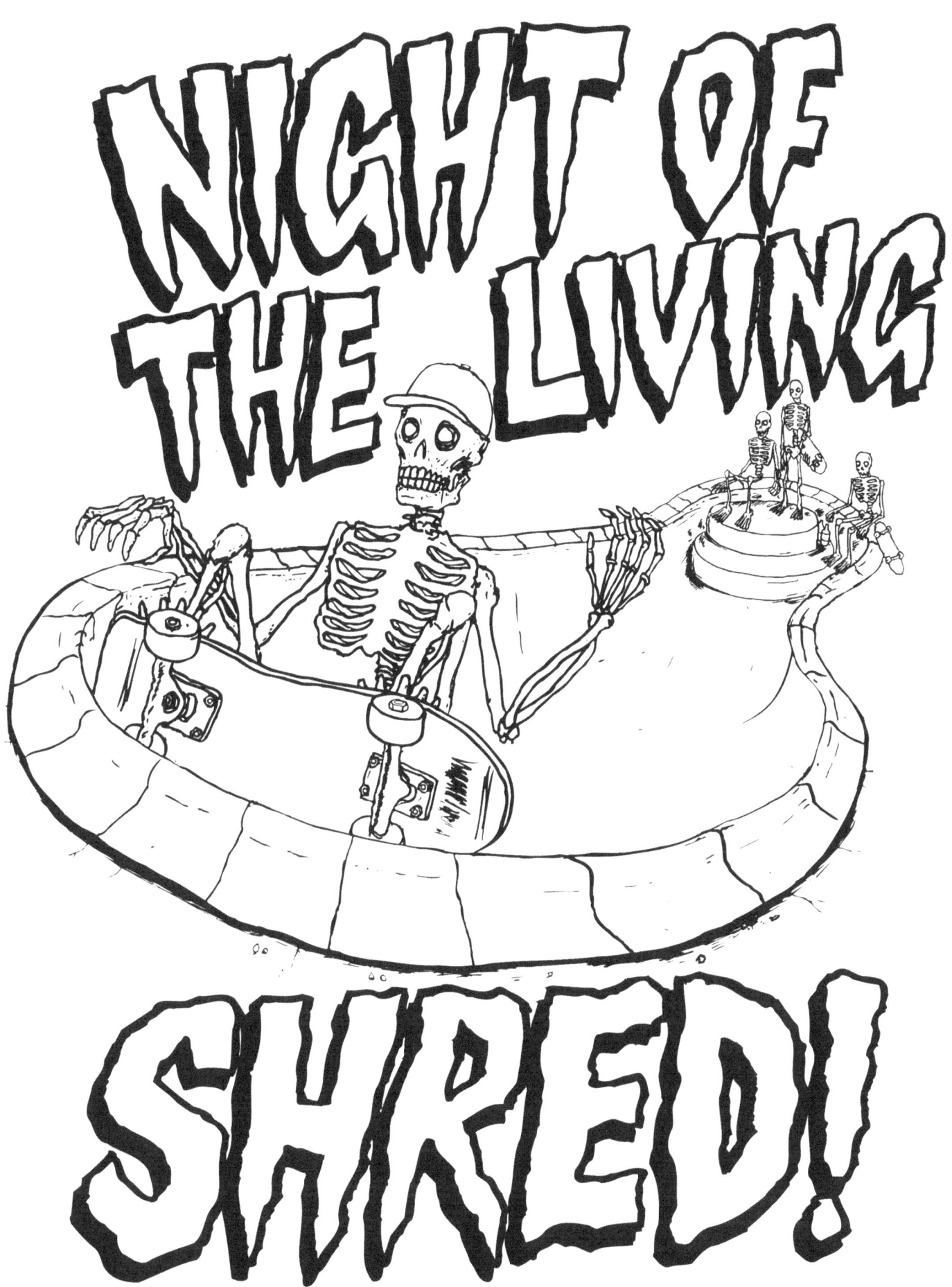

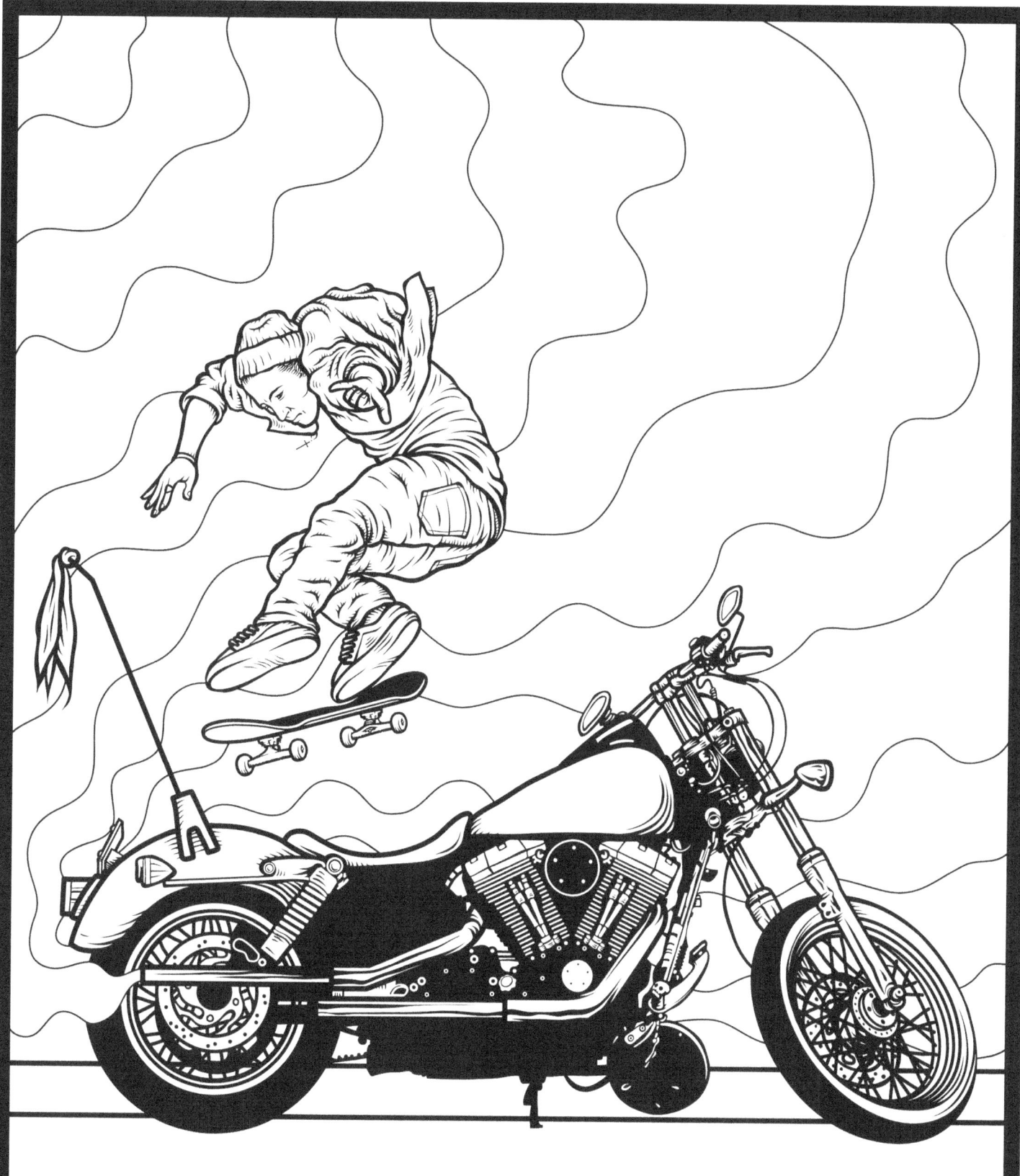

CHRIS BODIFORD
SAN DIEGO, CA

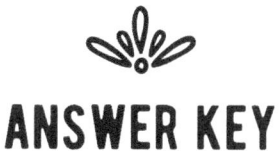

ANSWER KEY

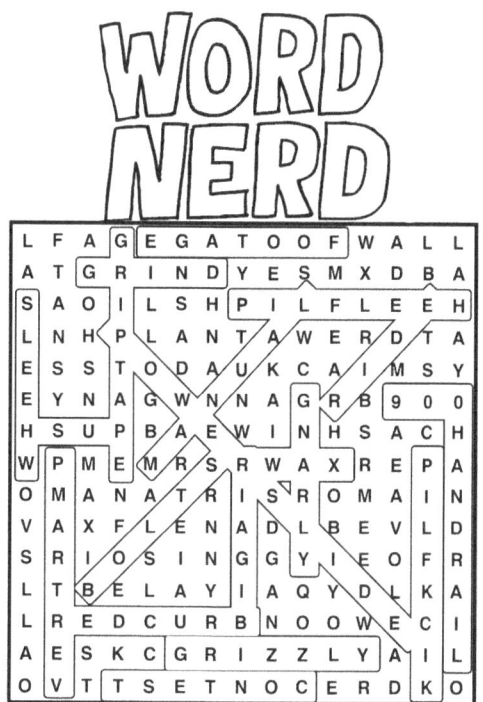

WORD NERD

L	F	A	G	E	G	A	T	O	O	F	W	A	L	L
A	T	G	R	I	N	D	Y	E	S	M	X	D	B	A
S	A	O	I	L	S	H	P	I	L	F	L	E	E	H
L	N	H	P	L	A	N	T	A	W	E	R	D	T	A
E	S	S	T	O	D	A	U	K	C	A	I	M	S	Y
E	Y	N	A	G	W	N	N	A	G	R	B	9	0	0
H	S	U	P	B	A	E	W	I	N	H	S	A	C	H
W	P	M	E	M	R	S	R	W	A	X	R	E	P	A
O	M	A	N	A	T	R	I	S	R	O	M	A	I	N
V	A	X	F	L	E	N	A	D	L	B	E	V	L	D
S	R	I	O	S	I	N	G	G	Y	I	E	O	F	R
L	T	B	E	L	A	Y	I	A	Q	Y	D	L	K	A
L	R	E	D	C	U	R	B	N	O	O	W	E	C	I
A	E	S	K	C	G	R	I	Z	Z	L	Y	A	I	L
O	V	T	T	S	E	T	N	O	C	E	R	D	K	O

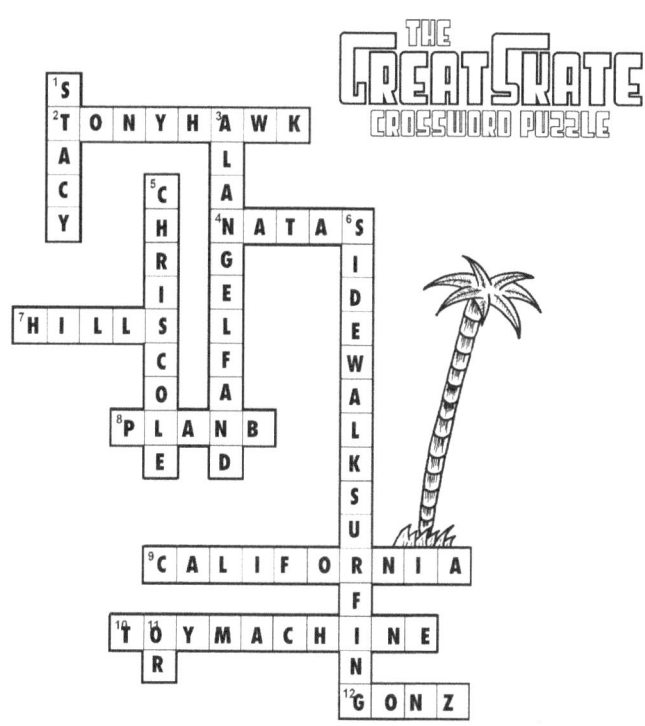

THE GREAT SKATE CROSSWORD PUZZLE

1. STACY
2. TONY HAWK
3. ANGELFAD
4. NATAS
5. CHRISCOE
6. SIDEWALKSURFIN
7. HILL
8. PLANB
9. CALIFORNIA
10. TOYMACHINE
11. GONZ

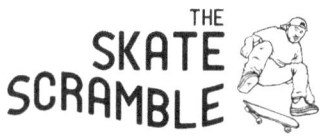

THE SKATE SCRAMBLE

UNSCRAMBLE THE SKATEPARK OBSTACLES

RAFBALT	FLATBAR
MPIYDAR	PYRAMID
MAIRNPMI	MINIRAMP
DEEGL	LEDGE
OBX	BOX
NLIARADH	HANDRAIL
IRSTSA	STAIRS
PHI	HIP
BUABH	HUBBA
WOBL	BOWL

Connect the dots to complete
Slash's beard

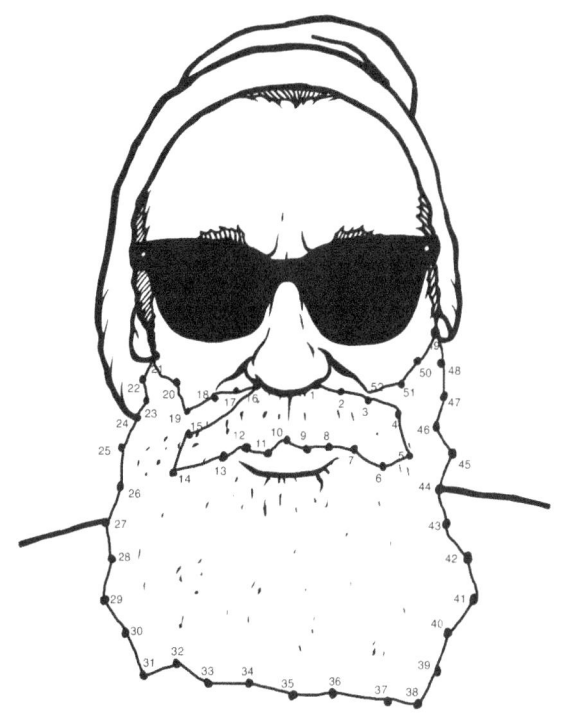

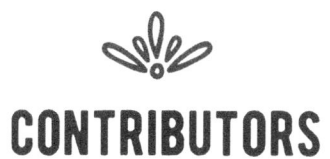

CONTRIBUTORS

SKATERS

TOM ASTA
GARRETT HILL
MANNY SANTIAGO
MIKEY TAYLOR
BRIAN 'SLASH' HANSEN

CHRIS BODIFORD
GANTRY HILL
MIKE MO CAPALDI
LIZZIE ARMANTO
RICHIE JACKSON

JON DICKSON
COREY DUFFEL
RYAN DECENZO

PHOTOGRAPHERS

CHAD FOREMAN
ATIBA JEFFERSON
JAMES RERES
BLAIR ALLEY
GANTRY HILL

FRANKIE MARTINEZ
NAMCHI VAN
JEREMY ADAMS
ANTHONY STULL
TY BUSH

ELMER BARRERO
DAVE CHAMI

ILLUSTRATORS

TODD BRATRUD
FOS
AYE JAY
ANDREW BRASWELL
ERIC ECKERT

BRAND SPONSORS

GLASSY SUNHATERS
HOTSHOT HANDLE
GRIZZLY GRIPTAPE
HELLACLIPS

METRO SKATEBOARDING
FORTUNE SKATEBOARDS
TRANSWORLD SKATEBOARDING

PRODUCERS

GANTRY HILL
GARRETT HILL
NADEEM MARC HADDAD

WRITERS

VIKTORIYA STOLITENKO